THE FORGOTTEN ART OF BUILDING AND USING A BRICK BAKE OVEN

A Practical Guide

by Richard M. Bacon

How to date, renovate, and use an existing brick oven and how to construct a new one from scratch.

Published MCMLXXVII by
YANKEE, INC.
Dublin, New Hampshire

This Book Has Been Prepared by the Staff of Yankee, Inc.:
Clarissa M. Silitch, Editor
Carl F. Kirkpatrick, Designer
Drawings and Diagrams by Margo Letourneau

First Edition

Library of Congress Catalog Card No. 77-74809

ISBN 0-911658-76-9

Dedicated To
Tim, Jamie, and Caroline
for bearing with their father's obsessions

ACKNOWLEDGMENTS

I would particularly like to thank the following people for their help during the preparation of this book:

Mr. Richard C. Borges, Curator, Strawbery Banke, Portsmouth, N.H.

Mr. David M. Hart, Director, Consulting Services, and Mr. Frederick C. Detwiller, Society for the Preservation of New England Antiquities, Boston, Mass.

Mr. Ralph Hodgkinson, retired, Director of "Crafts-at-Close-Range," Old Sturbridge Village, Sturbridge, Mass.

and their various staffs

And for their enduring patience in allowing me to wander in and out of their homes with measuring tape and questions,

Mr. and Mrs. Albert Aucoin

Mr. and Mrs. James C. Davis, Jr.

Mr. and Mrs. Robert Gregg

Mr. and Mrs. Murray Wigsten

CONTENTS

Foreword 8

Part 1: The Evolution of the Home-Use
Brick Bake Oven 10

Part 2: Technical Aspects of Brick Bake
Oven Construction 30

Part 3: Using the Brick Bake Oven 58

FOREWORD

The brick bake oven literally and figuratively occupied the central spot in the minds and homes of most early families. From its warm, dark recesses came forth the aroma of baking goodies; and sure enough, mouth-watering, crusty, browned delicacies, rolls and bread were pulled out with regularity. On "baking day" the members of the house gathered around and eagerly awaited the opportunity to "test" the delectable, soft-baked bread slathered with freshly churned butter.

Most of us modern-day folk have never even smelled bread being baked except when driving by a large commercial bakery, much less the aroma of bread baking in a brick oven. As a small child I can remember my Aunt Cassie baking bread, and also can recall the chewy texture, crispy crust and the marvelous, tasty, soft inside of each slice. I suppose I never gave the origin of this flavorful food a second thought. After all, usually one merely had to drive to the nearest store and pick a loaf from the rows and rows of similarly-shaped but differently colored packages lining the shelves. My aunt's bread was a distinctly rare treat. But even hers was baked in a new-fangled gas range, and lacked the taste of bread baked in an oven that had been fired with apple wood and other such varieties of fuel.

Lately we have had a large number of inquiries at the SPNEA* which relate to various aspects of using a brick bake oven. Many, many people are eager to try their hand at the ultimate in the make-your-own experience: baking in a brick oven.

*Society for the Preservation of New England Antiquities

However, the subject seems to be clouded with mystique; it seems that since this operation was so well known to the average household, even Fannie Farmer's grandmother never wrote a book about the subject. All homemakers learned their lessons early and well, and simple information on how and where to start the fire, when you know the oven is hot enough, how long to bake, and so on, is practically lost to history. In a similar fashion, questions relating to the repair and reconstruction of bake ovens went unanswered. Sources of plans, what bricks and mortar to use — these relatively simple techniques and materials were also lost to history. Unfortunately, there are few, if any, reliable sources one can be directed to for definitive answers.

Richard Bacon has, in this book, made some tremendous strides in allowing us to understand once again the bake oven. He has furnished us with practical information not only for building a bake oven, but also how to operate one. The book is a straightforward, well-documented work which traces the history of the bake oven in America and then outlines many of the types and styles in existence. He continues with up-to-date information on repairing and rebuilding an oven, and follows with operating techniques.

This book serves a dual purpose of providing much-needed scholarly information for use by the various professionals in the field, and at the same time gives the homeowner a reliable, practical source to help him rebuild and reuse a long-forgotten American art.

David M. Hart
Director, Consulting Services
Society for the Preservation of
New England Antiquities

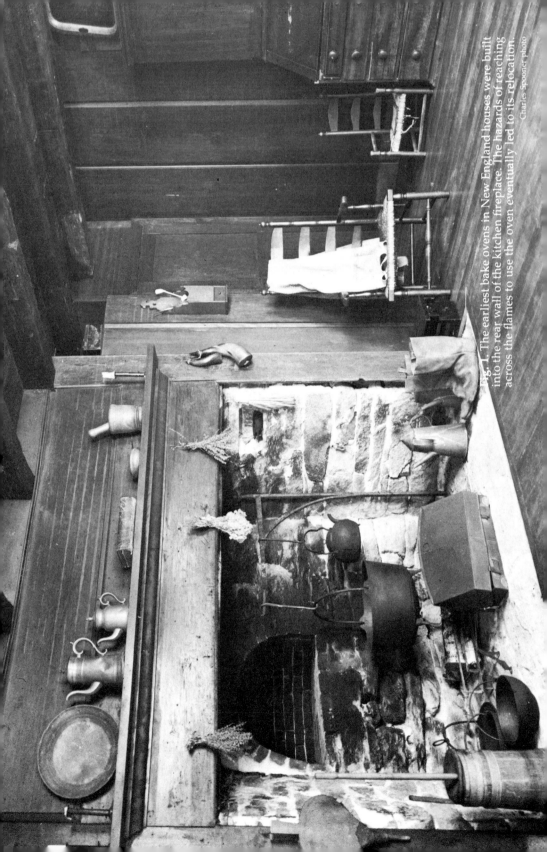

Fig. 1. The earliest bake ovens in New England houses were built into the rear wall of the kitchen fireplace. The hazards of reaching across the flames to use the oven eventually led to its relocation.

Charles Spooner photo

The Evolution of the Home-Use Brick Bake Oven 1

In most New England households — particularly in rural areas far from the coastal centers of wealth and fashion or where regional pride and habit continued to dictate the lifestyle — the wood-fired brick bake oven was an indispensable part of the kitchen from shortly after the time of settlement until as recently as a hundred years ago. Today, where homesteaders have an available supply of wood and the will to experiment with alternative ways of preparing food in an energy-threatened world, interest in the home bake oven is being rekindled. So, too, is the hunt for those once common cooking utensils — the spiders, rakes and trivets, salamanders, metal peels, tongs, cranes, pots, Dutch ovens and clockwork jacks — that were often essential when food was prepared over an open fire and in the adjacent bake oven.

The brick bake oven was a surprisingly simple structure for a mason to incorporate in the fireplace complex when a house was being built or renovated. It consisted of a flat hearth, coursed brick walls, a domed roof, and a rectangular or arched opening at the bottom of the front end to serve the double purpose of inserting and extracting fuel and food.

To learn to operate one effectively only required a supply of seasoned wood and time. Despite the many variations in size, location, and construction that can be seen in original home bake ovens in the northeast, the functional procedure for operating all of them is the same: build and maintain a fire on the oven hearth until the required temperature is reached, rake out the coals, insert prepared foods, and — while these cook — seal in the heat.

Both the steps and the basic design of the oven itself have hardly changed over the centuries since man first learned to bake in a preheated, self-radiating enclosure.

In hot climates, the bake oven of primitive cultures is still a semi-permanent, free-standing unit outdoors. Using the ground as the hearth, it is made with sun-dried adobe brick and plastered over with layers of mud or clay. While the isolated location helps disperse the heat generated in the firing up process, it also exposes the oven to weathering; therefore, repeated chinking with additional layers of mud is part of a standard maintenance program.

When early settlers first arrived in this country, they undoubtedly carried with them the knowledge of the wattle-and-clay-daub ovens they had left behind in northern Europe. Their design probably took its inspiration from an even older form — the beeskep or thatched beehive, a name by which it is still commonly known today. In the first settlements these were also isolated from the house because their wooden framework proved to be a fire hazard. Even if the wattles did not ignite as the oven was being heated, the greater fluctuations of New England weather created more problems. Layers of wet clay were continuously applied to the dome-shaped exterior to combat wind erosion, the freezing and thawing of water, and to help retain cooking heat. Because of their impermanence, none of those originally exposed bake ovens remains to be studied. A few, however, have been reconstructed in restored villages to help visitors recall some of the conditions under which the first arrivals to this country lived.

Because English immigrants to the southern Atlantic seaboard quickly found abundant claybanks, brick making there became an early Colonial industry. As a result, bake oven construction was more permanent and its operation less hazardous. Still isolated from the main house and operated under the prevailing plantation system, the oven was sheltered in an outbuilding where the numerous tasks of cooking for the household were concentrated.

From the middle-Atlantic states northwards — after the first decades of settlement — bake ovens were more apt to be built as a structural part of the masonry chimney in the house proper. Sometimes they were located in the gable end within the fireplace and, being deeper, often projected beyond the outside wall where their basic dome-shaped construction showed even though clayed or plastered over to retard erosion and retain heat.

In northern New England — where seasonal temperature variations are the greatest and heat from every available source must be utilized to help homesteaders get through the long winters more comfortably — the oven became part of the central masonry core that started in the cellar and ran up through the peak of the roof. This included most of the fireplaces and flues of the house. The oven hearth and domed roof were then concealed behind wooden or plastered partitions that divided the rooms. When the oven was in operation, this additional radiating heat was a further benefit once cold weather came.

There are bake ovens in New England and southwards that were built with field stone or dressed granite. As soon as brick making was an established industry, however, bricks became the more common construction material. Their regular shape made them easy to work with. They also responded more quickly to intense heat and continued to radiate it more effectively for longer periods. Kiln fired bricks often resist cracking and spalling more effectively than stone and even if they should powder or break after continuous use, they can be replaced more handily when the oven needs to be restored.

Dimensions of the brick bake oven were determined in part by the amount of space that could be devoted to it within the masonry core, by the changing needs of each household, and by the availability of workable building material. As families grew and households expanded, several bake ovens were often built under the same roof to meet seasonal demands and fluctuating numbers of people to be fed. A moderate-size oven in the kitchen was often suitable for daily family fare, but home production could be increased — or cooking activities transferred during hot summer months — by utilizing additional bake ovens in the hall, cellar, or ell.

Even the position of the kitchen bake oven in the chimney core shifted, as local masons and their apprentices expressed practical preferences for one location or another. Whether to build an oven into the right or left back wall of the kitchen fireplace — the position common in the earliest examples — or how to determine the height of the oven hearth from the floor may have been decided solely by their pragmatic diagnosis of the space they had to work with or by their experience and craftsmanship. It is interesting to speculate, however, that there must have been as many determined housewives in Colonial times as there are today who had an eye towards future convenience and efficiency rather than an ear towards rational argument as their bridal houses were being raised. Perhaps they could foresee — being strongly right- or left-handed themselves and of a certain build and stature — how to make the placement of the oven better suit their desires and, more to the point, how to convince the bricklayer to conform to them.

While studying or renovating an old house today, one is continuously struck by the ingenious and often flexible accomplishments of early masons. Variation on a simple theme was the rule. Many extant brick bake ovens have been rebuilt over the years to make necessary repairs, to reduce the size or change the shape, or to institute valid improvements in a constant process of modernizing cooking facilities. Some of these changes may have been from pure whimsey; others, to accommodate a new wife to the ways of an old house.

Those ovens that were successful in one house must often have been copied or adapted as more houses were built and communities expanded. Although brick bake ovens in any given area of New England may vary slightly in dimension, location, and structural technique, these are not as great as those from different regions. Some ovens have round hearths, broken only by the oven opening; others have deeper, oval floors. Some angle slightly to one side or the other. Many built in the mid-18th century have plastered façades or can be hidden by a raised panel or sheathed wooden door to keep them from sight when not in use. Much of this individuality depended on the skill of the craftsman — abetted by the housewife's suggestions — and on the means of the homeowner.

To a great extent marked similiarity of oven construction within a given area must be attributed to the work of a single master craftsman and his apprentices. Although their names may have been forgotten, the work of early craftsmen transmits an individuality and competence that mass production will never match.

Considering how common brick bake ovens are and how many were still in operation within the memories of people living today, it might seem surprising that no primer was published for a mason and his helpers (or indeed the homesteader himself) to follow while constructing them. None has yet been discovered by historians or the members of curatorial departments of restoration villages and museums. Aside from a few sparse references in household companion books and passing mention in rudimentary building manuals — some of which were reprinted as late as the 1860s and 1870s and at least give us an idea of how recent brick oven baking in the home was — their operation and construction apparently were so universally accepted as a part of daily living that no one thought of recording the information we find so lacking today. Perhaps this dearth of printed directions for a builder can also be accounted for by the lesser demands of a semi-literate society and by the basic strength of an apprentice system at a time when trade secrets were strongly guarded and a mason's helper worked long years to attain competence before his papers released him to accept commissions on his own. One can conclude that this body of knowledge was transmitted almost solely by oral tradition or was the result of individual observation, inventiveness, and a commonly shared experience.

From the mid-1600s — when the home bake oven was generally first incorporated in the central masonry core as a house was being built — until the end of the era of oven construction about two hundred years later, one can note several distinct stages of development in its normal evolutionary progress. For various reasons a great number of these changes occurred in the decades immediately following the American Revolution and foreshadowed the end of an era even while it was in its prime.

To try to date an old house, however, by the position and construction of its bake oven is a futile and inaccurate exercise today if only because of the time lag for current fashions and newer techniques to take hold — particularly as one moves farther inland and down the economic ladder.

Change came slowly and erratically to rural areas in the days before mass communication.

Whereas most New England communities can still boast of several substantial houses built by people of local importance from the mid-18th century onwards that reflect the more refined architectural styles and prevailing contemporary fashions of wealthier coastal regions, the majority of homes in all villages were working farmhouses until fairly recently. Their owners had limited means and little awareness of changing trends, however comfortably they may have lived on a barter system economy. The presence in a house of one type of brick bake oven from an earlier period may not establish the age of that house but merely indicate an era. It may also show the preference of a mason or homeowner who felt comfortable with a familiar and time-honored design. Conversely, later styles of oven construction in an older house are often the result of innovations carried out long after the house was built. Both can mislead today's antiquarian. To date an oven, in addition to its position, one should also take into account the size, type, and composition of the bricks themselves, analyze the kind and color of the mortar used, and be aware of a variety of typical pointing techniques — especially when renovating an existing oven. Even with such accumulated knowledge — and no definite proof in the form of written deeds or records to corroborate it — such observations can only serve as a guide in estimating the age of a house.

Still, one can learn a lot from the study of old brick bake ovens and set some broad time spans which at least mark the appearance of different positions and use of newer techniques.

From already documented houses historians agree that the earliest bake ovens in the home were incorporated in New England houses in the mid-17th century and were constructed in the rear wall of the kitchen fireplace either to the right or left of the smoke channel. At that time the kitchen fireplace was cavernous. Reflecting its medieval origin in northern Europe, it was deep, high, and box-like in appearance. The lintel — often just below the ceiling — was of such gigantic thickness and length that it could easily span the width of a chimney and support the weight of stone or brick masonry above it. These early ovens — and there are examples where two were built side-by-side in the back wall — as well as later variations when the oven was moved to one or the other angled covings as the design of the fireplace evolved, shared a common flue (Figs. 1 and 2). When a fire was built in the oven, the smoke and flames shot out its mouth and were drawn directly up the central chimney. Live coals and ashes were raked out onto the floor of the fireplace, food inserted in the oven cavity, and a cover propped against the opening. The earliest covers were probably boards with a wooden handle centered on the outside surface. Metal was a rare and expensive item. Later, even with the oven in this position, a local craftsman or perhaps the home-owner himself — who was apt to be a jack-of-all-trades — fashioned a fitted oven cover from forged iron or lined the

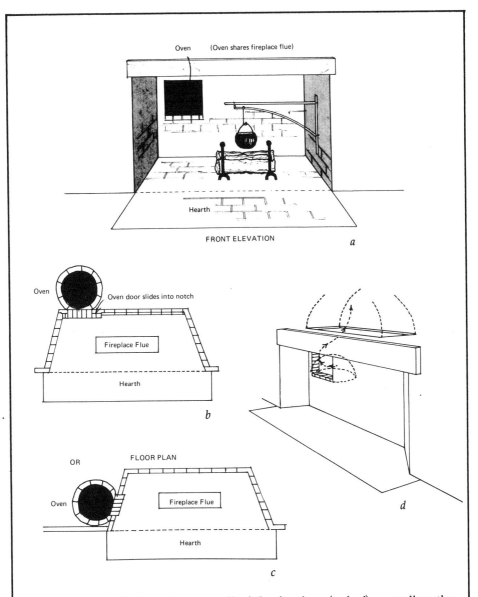

Fig. 2. Ovens built into the rear wall of the fireplace (*a, b, d*), as well as the slightly later version located in one of the angled covings (*c*), shared the fireplace flue.

17

wooden board with a sheet of metal to make it more permanent. This door slid into a vertical groove between the bricks in front of the oven opening and was anchored against the facing bricks to seal in the heat when baking.

To reach across a hearth fire — which was kept as much for heat as for cooking — or among kettles of boiling water (at first suspended from lug poles in the chimney flue and later from swinging iron cranes) in order to use the oven was hazardous. Death or maiming by fire and scalding water took a toll of Colonial cooks second only to death by childbirth.

Two advantages the position of this bake oven offered, however, were that a common flue could be used by both oven and fireplace — thus cutting down additional construction time and material — and that live coals could be raked directly onto the hearth when the oven was ready to be cleaned and sealed. Harmless ashes from these fires were later transferred to a dry storage area and saved.

This type of self-contained oven was typical of the 17th and early 18th centuries. The oven hearth and its beehive dome might run straight back into the masonry core or curve either to the right or left depending whether it was constructed into the back wall or into one of the covings.

By the mid-1700s a general trend appeared — corresponding to specific structural changes — in the first major relocation of the home bake oven.

By then bake ovens were positioned in the right or left fireplace jambs or shoulders — that vertical masonry area on either side of the hearth which forms the front of the coving and is built parallel to the fireplace wall facing the room. This brought the oven away from and to one side of the hearth fire and at the same time often raised it to a more convenient height from the floor (Fig. 3). Tending the bake oven was safer and easier in this position. It was no longer necessary to reach across flames to use the oven.

However, in this new location several structural changes were required. At about this time the kitchen fireplace was evolving on its own into a shallower, lower cavity with its coving more angled to the back wall. This gave it a less severe rectangular appearance than its medieval forerunner and promoted a more efficient use of reflected heat. Nevertheless, both the jamb in which

18

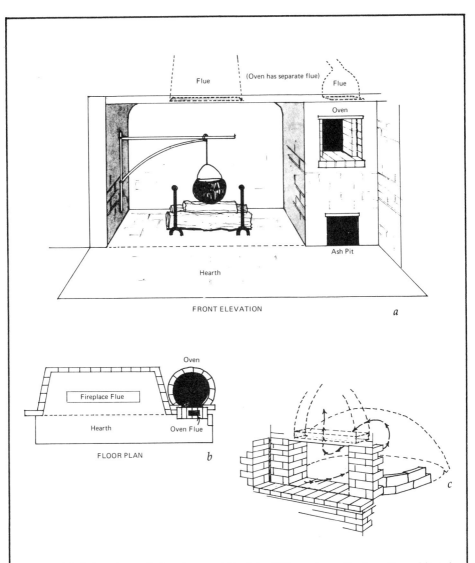

Flue

(Oven has separate flue)

Flue

Oven

Ash Pit

Hearth

FRONT ELEVATION

a

Oven

Fireplace Flue

Hearth

Oven Flue

FLOOR PLAN

b

c

Fig. 3. With fireplaces dating from mid to late 18th-century, the hearth and lintel are extended to accommodate the brick oven now built into one of the fireplace jambs. This new position necessitated a separate oven flue, which was angled in to join that of the fireplace (*a, b*). In diagram *c*, the oven is recessed in from the front plane of the jamb, providing a shelf for the separate oven door, one edge of which fits into the notch shown shaded to the left of the opening.

the oven was constructed and the hearth before it had to be broadened to accommodate the new location and guard against falling sparks when the oven fire was kindled or live coals transferred to the fireplace hearth. This new position automatically off-centered the fireplace opening in the wall. The hearth was extended either by adding another granite slab in line with the one already existing or — more often in the case of renovation than new construction — laying additional bricks in a continuing pattern to form the extended hearth. There are several examples which show that the fireplace at one point was actually torn apart and rebuilt in smaller proportions so as to make room for a wider jamb to accommodate a new oven without having to extend the original hearthstones.

More fundamental than these alterations, however, was the necessity of a smaller second vent. Facing the room adjacent to the fireplace as it now did, the oven could no longer share the fireplace flue.

An oven vent was built in front of and directly above the oven opening which was usually recessed about eight inches — the length of a common brick — from the front plane of the jamb. The flue opening was four inches deep and nearly as wide (from twelve to sixteen inches) as the oven opening itself. This was built vertically behind the chimney breast, then angled in to join the fireplace flue at about ceiling height. A portable door was anchored and propped in a vertical slot at one side of the oven opening while it was in operation (as was done in the earlier position) between this and the flue or set and braced against a half-inch brick lip that had been left on both sides of the oven opening.

In brick bake ovens of this type and position — generally from the mid to late 18th century and even into the 1900s in more rural areas — there was no attempt to incorporate a damper in this flue. This omission was not unusual in the days before central heating. Even the early fireplaces were without them. Homesteaders depended on a constant fire most of the year both for cooking and heat. Besides, the only lightweight, non-flammable material that could possibly serve as a damper in the days before the American Revolution was forged iron. This was too costly for most colonists to contemplate using in a chimney. During the summertime, in rooms that did not require fires, many inventive Yankees made fireboards to block the fireplace openings. These cut down drafts and rain. They also discouraged invasion of insects, birds, and small rodents down the open chimney. In the core of the household the cook and her helpers had to learn to adapt. The absence of dampers was one of the realities of living.

This scarcity of iron also dictated the construction of lintels in early fireplaces and brick ovens. The lintel is a horizontal, load-bearing, structural member which spans the top of an opening whether fireplace, oven, door, or window. It must be sufficiently strong to support weight from above; otherwise, it will sag and may eventually crumble or break. Since a course of horizontally laid pieces of masonry — unsupported from below or within — cannot by itself withstand this kind of pressure, other materials and techniques were substituted to provide essential support.

One was the stout wooden beam — usually oak — already mentioned. This was embedded at each end in the masonry at the top of the fireplace jambs. Another was a split stone which could be of smaller dimensions, yet support heavier loads than a wooden beam.

Whereas both of these — scaled down — could have met the structural requirements as a lintel for the brick oven, the former would not be safe. When the oven fire is kindled, flames shoot under the lintel which spans the oven opening and are drawn around it directly up the flue. Any unchecked fire can raze the house. Early masons, therefore, depended mostly on split stone — often granite where available — as their only choice of a non-flammable lintel in the absence of iron to span the oven opening. This could then support courses of brick laid above it.

Or, they turned to an ancient practice and constructed a small bricked arch. While this may, in fact, have allowed for the easier passage of food and fuel into the oven, it was more likely used because the arch gives great strength to masonry construction without the aid of additional support. Each brick is angled in such a way that the stress of weight from above is equally shared and the arch will not collapse.

Where a forged iron bar was available even as early as the mid-18th century — and one sometimes sees a piece that had originally been fashioned for an altogether different purpose and then, inventively used to support either the fireplace or bake oven lintel, or both, in an era when recycling material at hand was the normal practice among frugal New Englanders — this provided support for the bricked courses above it. Iron was both in fact and in appearance a lighter method of construction than either an oak beam or split stone.

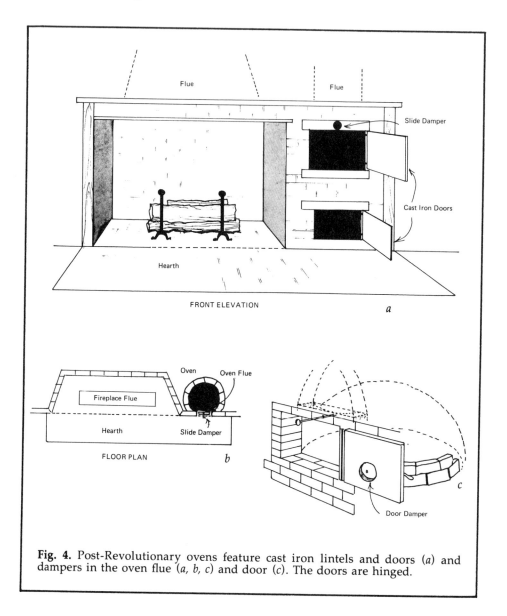

Fig. 4. Post-Revolutionary ovens feature cast iron lintels and doors (*a*) and dampers in the oven flue (*a, b, c*) and door (*c*). The doors are hinged.

A third progression in the evolution of the brick bake oven came after the American War of Independence and corresponded with the introduction of cast iron manufactured on this side of the Atlantic. This was cheaper, stronger, and more easily produced on a large scale than forged iron. Coincidentally, it was only one of several developments — begun in England as the Industrial Revolution in the last half of the 18th century and fostered here as one of many native industries after the political ties had been broken — that catapulted the western world into modern times.

It also foreshadowed the end of brick oven construction and use in American homes. As accelerating steps were taken to make cooking more efficient in the decades immediately before and after the turn of the century, the bake oven as it had existed for centuries became only one of an increasing number of casualties although its final demise was still a long way off.

The brick bake oven within the chimney complex remained in the same position — in the jamb to one side of the kitchen fireplace — but several modifications were possible once cast iron became so readily available (Fig. 4). These all made it easier to operate.

Now an iron frame and hinged door could be cast to cover the oven opening. These were mass produced in standard sizes and installed by the mason flush with the brick facing of the fireplace jamb. It meant, however, because the oven flue remained sandwiched between the mouth of the oven and this protective door, that a damper became essential for the first time. Without it — once the oven had been prepared — there would be no way for the cook to retain the heat while food was baking. Therefore, a solid piece of cast iron was laid horizontally in the oven flue to block the bottom of the vent. Its perimeter was supported by a lip of bricks prepared by the mason. This slid from front to rear in the flue and was operated with a thin iron strap riveted to the center of the near side of the damper plate, inserted through a small rectangular opening in the top of the cast iron door frame, and usually capped with a knob which projected into the room, above the oven door. To allow passage of smoke up the vent, the damper handle was pulled out; to retain heat in the oven, it was pushed in. A sliding or crescent-shaped draft regulator was also incorporated in the bottom of the cast iron door itself so the cook could control combustion in the oven. By adjusting both of these devices, the cook could exercise some degree of remote control without having to open the oven door so frequently.

These innovations certainly made home baking in the wood-fired oven both cleaner and safer. Although the process of using the oven remained the same as it had been for centuries, this type of invention made possible by the introduction of a new kind of material paved the way for all sorts of modifications that continue to change cooking habits even in today's kitchens.

Before discussing further the increasingly rapid changes made in the brick bake oven in the name of progress, some attention should be given another integral part of the chimney complex.

This is the ash pit (Fig. 5). Some historians doubt that the fundamental use of this bricked cave which regularly appears in conjunction with the bake oven on or just above hearth level and directly below the oven was for the storage of ashes. Alternative uses proposed, however, are also debatable.

Certainly in the earliest mid-17th century examples of the brick oven, there is no ash pit. The reason for this may be obvious: live coals were raked directly onto the fireplace hearth where they joined the accumulating residue of ashes from the hearth fire. Later, when the ashes were cold and threatened to occupy too much space, they were transferred to a dry storage area to be saved. Collection of wood ashes was an important aspect of Colonial life. Ashes were regularly used in the home manufacture of lye, one of the chief ingredients in soap making, mordanting wool for dyeing, and processing corn. Ashes also contain the important chemical *potash*, an invaluable fertilizer, and *pearl ash*, an early form of baking soda, obtained principally from apple-wood ash.

From the time the bake oven was relocated to one of the fireplace jambs, the ash pit generally made its first appearance as part of the masonry complex. An ash pit dating from this period usually has an opening narrower than that of the oven itself but is equally deep. The floor and walls are bricked. The roof of the ash pit is either a large, single flat stone (which supports the bricked hearth of the bake oven above it) or two or more longer split granite slabs, the ends of which rest on the walls of the pit. These, in turn, are overlaid with brick to form the oven hearth.

Since variety marks much of this kind of construction in the home by regional masons or the homeowner himself, the difficulty or expense of procuring suitable flat stones or split granite in

Fig. 5. *Above* — Ash pit serving a middle-period (*c.* 1780) recessed brick oven. Note stabilizing notch for oven door to right of oven. *Below* — Late-period (*c.* 1849) fireplace-oven-ash pit complex, showing iron lintel and hinged oven door with damper, also an iron fireplace damper handle set in the panel above the mantel.

Stephen T. Whitney photos

a given area may have accounted for the substitution of wooden planks for stone. However, when live coals were inadvertently stored in this cavity under the oven, it could have been disastrous, and to judge from the evidence, apparently often was. Although there are some rare examples of ash pits which contain a separate flue through which heat and gases can be vented to the outdoors, for the most part these pits were self-contained. This may account for the extreme charring on the underside of the planks one sees in many extant bricked ash pits. Often, when used as an expedient storage area for glowing coals, the planking has burned through and collapsed, dragging the brick oven hearth with it into the pit. Occasionally, fire could also have spread undetected from above through unpointed joints in the oven hearth. The result would have been the same. The only remedy for such a situation was to rebuild the entire component to render it safe to use.

One of the most practical designs for an ash pit is found in the fireplace complex at the Walsh House (1796) at Strawbery Banke, Portsmouth, New Hampshire. Here, a square opening was left in the center of the ash pit floor and connects with a bricked chute that funnels ashes to the cellar. This innovation adds convenience as well as safety. Live coals from the oven and fireplace can be banked around the perimeter of the ash pit floor. When all the life has gone out of them, they are raked down the chute and collected without effort in a container in the cellar.

The self-contained ash pit which has no vent or chute may have been used for other purposes. Some contend that it was primarily intended as a storage place for kindling or split, dry wood for oven fires. If so, it is too small, hard to reach, and could be a possible fire threat. Others say that it housed utensils that were only occasionally needed for cooking on the adjacent hearth. To find what was wanted at the proper time would have meant rummaging in a dark tunnel — particularly inconvenient in the days before battery-powered flashlights. Finally, some theorize that this cavity was intended only as a place to keep foods warm or to store them away from domestic animals but the partition between the ash pit and fireplace coving and the thickness of the roof which supports the oven hearth both prohibit heat from passing through the bricks.

Whatever its intended use — and a storage place for ashes still seems the most logical — the fact is that these masonry caves do exist in many, but not all, old houses today in conjunction with a bake oven. They usually also have a cover similar to that used on the oven. Their inclusion in the chimney complex (and sometimes even the construction of a second niche between it and the oven proper) at least allowed the oven hearth to be raised to a convenient height from the floor (about thirty inches) and contributed an additional advantage: built-in space cuts the cost and need for material. Because many bricks were laboriously kiln-fired right on the property at the time of construction, this was an advantage Yankees were not likely to overlook.

In the last decades of the 18th century and immediately thereafter, several more innovations were attempted in an effort to make food preparation increasingly efficient and convenient. None of them became popular over a widespread area.

In one experiment the oven flue was moved back to the top of the beehive dome. The lower opening became a firebox. Heat and smoke were vented around the beehive walls between the oven and a masonry shell. Sliding dampers and draft regulators were used to control combustion and heat retention. This called for a continuous fire during baking and constant adjustments. Unfortunately, heat could not be evenly distributed within the oven by this method.

But it did mark the dawn of an age of mechanical and technical advances in the kitchen. Combined with the availability of cast iron and the gradual introduction of anthracite coal rather than wood as fuel in the more highly concentrated urban areas, American inventiveness began to come of age in the first glow of freedom. The rapid changes that now occurred were soon to revolutionize households throughout New England.

The strangely disturbed expatriate genius Count Rumford — born Benjamin Thompson in Woburn, Massachusetts, in 1753 — was one of those who led the way (see *The Forgotten Art of Building a Good Fireplace* by Vrest Orton, Yankee, Inc., 1969). His tour of Bavarian military establishments in the late 1700s focused his attention towards what went on in the kitchen. Ultimately, his invention the "Rumford Roaster" did more to modernize institutional cooking of the time than to improve the housewife's lot, but the inventions of Rumford, Benjamin Franklin, and others of the post-Revolutionary period speeded changes in the American home and kitchen. Built-in cast iron cooking ranges had their day.

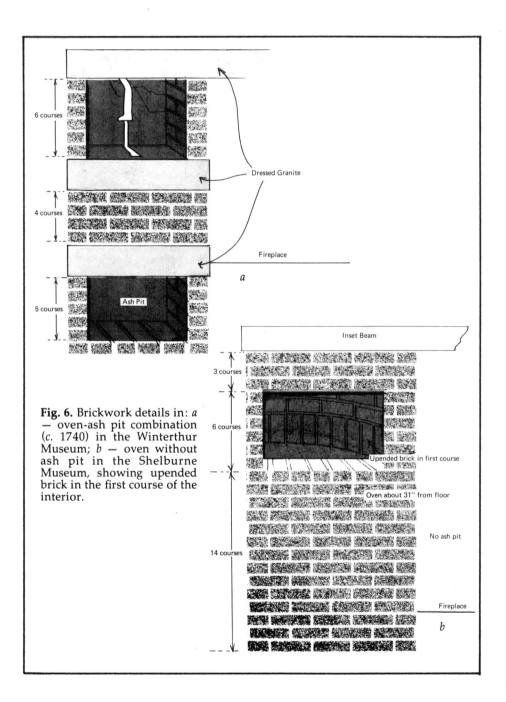

6 courses

Dressed Granite

4 courses

Fireplace

a

Ash Pit

5 courses

Inset Beam

3 courses

6 courses

Upended brick in first course

Oven about 31″ from floor

No ash pit

14 courses

Fireplace

b

Fig. 6. Brickwork details in: *a* — oven-ash pit combination (*c.* 1740) in the Winterthur Museum; *b* — oven without ash pit in the Shelburne Museum, showing upended brick in the first course of the interior.

28

In 1845 Harper and Brothers of New York published "Webster's Domestic Economy and Housekeeping" — a book which included general arrangements of a "modern" kitchen and pictured an iron and masonry complex built along an entire kitchen wall and which, for the first time perhaps, could justifiably be called the "food preparation center". It contained a range with an oven on one side and a boiler on the other, recesses to accommodate a hot plate, sets of steam tables, warming ovens, etc.

For people of average means in rural mid-19th century New England, however, it was not the iron range but the cast iron cookstove (combining a firebox, bake oven, cooking surface with removable lids, warming ovens, and hot water reservoir in one free-standing unit) that most generally affected domestic change. It aided cooking and provided supplemental heat. The wood- or coal-burning cast iron stove was easier to operate, cleaner, safer, less time-consuming, and more efficient than the kitchen fireplace and its abutting brick bake oven. It was quick to install and cancelled the need for a ponderous masonry core through which to vent it to the outdoors. It also served as a symbol. Such domestic innovations — ever closer to the reach of an increasingly affluent population — reinforced the pride of a young nation with time to devote to pursuits other than war and mere survival. Symbolically, inventions like the stove seemed to cleave a Colonial past from a progressive, independent future.

With the coming of the stove, the brick bake oven and wood-gorging kitchen fireplace were frequently sealed up and plastered over to serve only as semi-permanent repositories for the cast-off artifacts of a bygone age. Often, the entire masonry core was dismantled during renovations of old houses and the bricks used to construct the single flues to accommodate cookstoves and heating stoves in less space.

Ironically, like the snail which has slithered through time unchanged, the brick bake oven might have gone on forever performing its simple and necessary function. Progress intervened. Normal evolution in man's quest for solutions doomed it. Political and economic freedom coincided with a great technical awakening at the dawn of the 19th century. In today's kitchens we are still feeling those repercussions: increasing mechanization and ever advancing technology still threaten to transform cooking from an art to a science.

Fig. 7. By careful attention to all details of construction, a modern mason can renovate an existing brick oven and make it safe for baking once again. When not in use, this oven complex was concealed by the panelled wooden door shown open behind the mason.

L. F. Willard photo

Technical Aspects of Brick Bake Oven Construction 2

Brick bake ovens were usually built — as they still are today — to the requirements of the individual site rather than from a common blueprint. They were constructed either by an energetic householder with a knack for working with brick and mortar and the ability to copy a nearby example, or by a reputable mason and his apprentice whose wider experience and knowledge were called upon from time to time by members of an expanding society as new houses were raised or old ones renovated. A man known for a variety of practical skills — and who could point to examples of his work locally — could probably have kept himself in jobs for a lifetime without ever having to specialize. Those whose talents lay in working with masonry — both stone and brick — often established reputations within a limited radius from their home and were frequently occupied laying foundations, building retaining walls, paving cellars, erecting stone or brick outbuildings, or raising a central chimney. Such men could also construct a brick bake oven.

However much the results vary from one local area of New England to the next, there are many structural points all successful brick bake ovens have in common. By studying examples from the past and noting how they were constructed and what materials were used, the modern mason can duplicate the simple beehive form and build a contemporary oven that is equally functional; or he can renovate an existing oven and make it safe to cook in again.

Much of the variety of extant brick bake ovens comes both from the abilities of the mason who built them and from their placement within the chimney complex. Those in the rear wall or either of the covings of the kitchen fireplace should be the least complicated to copy today in a newly-conceived house with a large central chimney because they will not call for the construction of either a separate flue or an ash pit. Before choosing this type, however, remember a lesson from history: this is potentially the most hazardous to operate because unless the fireplace is of abnormal width the cook will be too close to the hearth fire for safety. It will also be dark and less convenient. In addition, the selection of this early type of oven position will expand the sheer size and bulk of the chimney core and influence the placement and construction of other fireplaces and flues in adjacent rooms.

Any of the later styles of brick ovens will be more challenging to build but safer to operate. When an oven is built into one of the fireplace jambs, it will not only require a flue of its own but — depending on whether the oven is recessed from the jamb or brought out flush to it — may involve installing a damper as well as mortaring in a cast iron frame and hinged door.

While the project is still in the planning stage, the builder must also decide if he wants to include an ash pit in the overall design. This can be useful and authentic; it can also save bricks.

Assuming that the homeowner of today is interested in constructing a functional brick bake oven which he can use as an alternative method of preparing food either occasionally or for extended periods of time, one of his chief concerns should be for safety — both for the cook and for the house. Special problems will arise when renovating an old oven to make it safe to operate. If one cannot solve these himself, it would be better to abandon the project altogether or to call in experts who can.

Building a Brick Bake Oven Today

After deciding on the design and position of his brick bake oven, the modern homeowner must then consider the two essential materials he will be working with — bricks and mortar.

Apparently, there are more schools of thought concerning the proper way of matching and mixing these ingredients than there are practicing masons. Agreement among them is as hard to find as it is among diplomats. Those interested primarily in preservation and conservation work advocate one approach based on observation of how brick bake ovens were bonded in the past. They reinforce this by scientific analysis of brick and mortar composition in a modern laboratory. Others, interested more in functionalism perhaps than in either authenticity or aesthetic con-

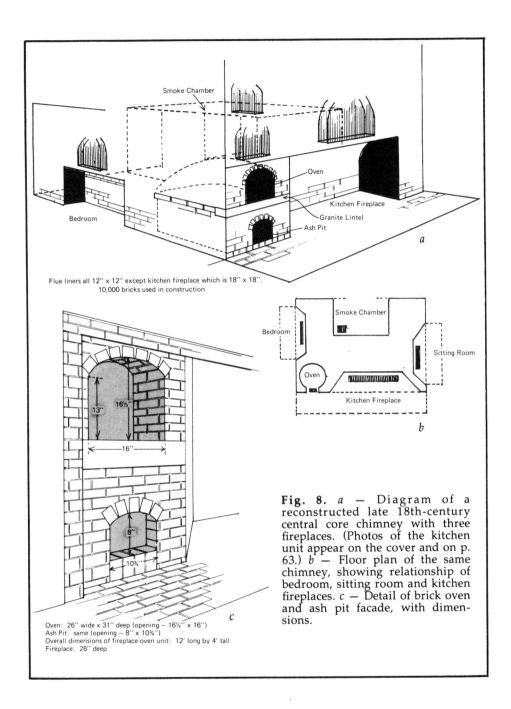

Smoke Chamber

Oven

Kitchen Fireplace

Granite Lintel

Ash Pit

Bedroom

a

Flue liners all 12″ x 12″ except kitchen fireplace which is 18″ x 18″.
10,000 bricks used in construction

Smoke Chamber

Bedroom

Sitting Room

Oven

Kitchen Fireplace

b

16½″

13″

16″

8″

10¾″

c

Oven: 26″ wide x 31″ deep (opening — 16½″ x 16″)
Ash Pit: same (opening — 8″ x 10¾″)
Overall dimensions of fireplace-oven unit: 12′ long by 4′ tall
Fireplace: 28″ deep

Fig. 8. *a* — Diagram of a reconstructed late 18th-century central core chimney with three fireplaces. (Photos of the kitchen unit appear on the cover and on p. 63.) *b* — Floor plan of the same chimney, showing relationship of bedroom, sitting room and kitchen fireplaces. *c* — Detail of brick oven and ash pit facade, with dimensions.

33

siderations, may champion a different set of standards based on experience and what apparently works. Much of this controversy centers around the use of hard or soft brick in the construction of an oven.

One common assertion linking both extremes is that when masonry work is to be used in conjunction with intense heat — such as in an oven or fireplace — the hardness of the brick should be matched to the hardness of the mortar used to bond them.

This is based on the fact that unusual thermal extremes affect the rates of expansion and contraction of the materials used. If brick and mortar expand and contract at even rates together, cracks along the joints and in the bricks themselves can be minimized with a little forethought.

Types of Brick

Essentially, there are three types of brick available for today's mason. *Firebrick,* a modern cream-colored product of larger than normal proportions than either of the other two, is used in many fireboxes and kilns but rarely — both for appearance and cost — in brick bake oven and home fireplace construction. They are almost crumbly in their consistency and are made from a special fire clay.

More common are both *hard* and *soft* brick. The major difference between them is their consistency. This is determined by their position in the kiln during the firing process. Soft brick came from the top of the Colonial kiln; hard brick from nearer the heat source.*

Either a consistently high heat intensity was not possible to maintain throughout the kiln when wood was the universal fuel — particularly when many of the bricks were produced on the home place at the site of construction and in local brickyards where quality control fluctuated enormously — or a particular composition of brick was wanted for a specific job.

Hard brick is heavier, denser, and stronger. In the extreme it often has a glazed appearance. Because of its composition, this type of brick is more impervious to the effects of weathering and to ranges of hot and cold. In early times it was more costly to buy because there were fewer manufactured, and they were more fuel-

*See "Making and Firing Weatherproof Bricks," *The Forgotten Arts, Book Three,* Yankee, Inc., 1976, p.45.

consuming to produce. Until well into the 19th century when technology affected changes in commercial brick making, hard brick manufacture lagged behind production of soft brick. For these reasons, therefore, those hard bricks that were available despite increased cost were used where they would do the most good: in exterior walls and in chimney construction only from the peak of the roof upwards. Being a clay product, brick is more susceptible to water erosion than to normal temperature variations. The constant freezing and thawing of water particles which permeate both brick and mortared joints will eat away and eventually disintegrate both masonry and mortar unless a constant maintenance program is followed. Some extremely soft, unburned brick from the 17th century have been found to absorb as much as 35% of their weight in water, whereas modern hard brick will take in less than 3%. (For those who have had the experience of laying a brick walk outdoors — either in sand or embedded in cement — using a variety of old bricks, the properties of these two kinds will be obvious: after just one winter soft brick will have cracked and even pulverized; hard brick will retain its form more consistently.)

Soft brick — because it is more porous and less dense — was reserved for construction that would not be exposed to high humidity and rain or snow. Great quantities of soft bricks were used to build interior walls, fireplaces, and bake ovens. Soft brick and broken brick were also used as filler in those areas of the structure that could not be seen.

Today, some masons and historical preservationists maintain that only soft brick was used in building a bake oven because the composition of the fired clay allowed a better retention of heat than hard brick even though over a long period of time and great usage, you could expect them to disintegrate and, therefore, have to be replaced more frequently. They also note that a soft mortar — commonly known as lime mortar — had quickly followed the use of pure clay as a bonding material, and this had an expansion and contraction rate similar to that of the soft brick.

Types of Mortar

Many old chimneys and ovens found today are still mortared with clay. This was a common practice in the early 17th century — even well into the 19th century in inland areas — and probably accounts for the destruction by fire of many of the original settlers' houses. Fire can eat through weak joints and spread unseen to wooden partitions. Although this mortaring practice certainly poses a threat to both lives and buildings today and should be thoroughly investigated by anyone renovating an old house before the chimney is used, over the years — where the joints have not been exposed to water and high humidity — the clay itself, having been constantly baked by the heat of the fire, often remains as durable now as it was shortly after being applied.

With the discovery of limestone sources in this country, mortaring practices changed. One source was the heaps of shells left by the Indians in coastal regions. Farther inland natural deposits of "limerock" (limestone or marble) were discovered. Both of these had first to be burned ("quicklime") and then slaked with water ("hydrated lime"). Early methods were primitive and the product full of impurities. Slaked lime could be used by mixing it with appropriate amounts of sand and water — the proportions of which varied depending on local custom and the mason's experience — and this used to bond bricks together. Because of the lime, joints in brick and stonework were light in color — a characteristic today's conservationists like to duplicate with more modern products to attain a degree of authenticity. Because it was impure, lime mortar also often contained a portion of natural cements. While these provided added strength, this type of early mortar was essentially soft — actually not completely hardening for several years — and frequently deteriorated more rapidly than the masonry units themselves. If used on exterior walls where joints are exposed to weathering, the lime eventually may leach out, weakening the bond and streaking the brickwork.

Technology has developed other mortars that are more pure, stronger, and longer lasting.

Lump lime (bought by the barrelful by masons and plasterers as late as the 1930s) could be used by those who wanted to mix their own mortars with sand, natural cements, and water for masonry work. However, it is no longer available on the market today. A later product, mason's lime, is. This does not have a large following although it is more refined than its predecessor. It is added to masonry cement to affect the workability of the mortar, the color, vary the strength, and to stretch amounts and cut costs.

Two types of cement dominate today's market. Masonry cement is a commercial product manufactured specifically for use with bricks and stones. This contains amounts of Portland cements, lime, and fillers pre-mixed by formula by each manufacturing company. The mason combines this with fine sand and water on the job and sometimes adds additional amounts of lime. Both light and dark masonry cements are available.

The second is Portland cement which was developed in the late 19th century. This is occasionally used by masons in conjunction with brick work but because — when mixed with an aggregate — it is intended to withstand particularly heavy loads and stresses; it is mostly used for laying footings, foundations, piers, and pads — not for masonry work. When masons do use it, they also use hard brick so that the coefficient of expansion and contraction will be similar. Some masons add significant amounts of Portland cement to their regular masonry cement mixtures on the theory that it provides that much more strength. This practice is based only on individual experience and is often only a local custom.

For those particularly interested in restoration work, care should be taken to study bonding already between the brick joints so that a mortar of the same composition can be made for new patchwork. A soft mortar will crumble and sometimes dissolve in water; a hard mortar (like one made with Portland cement) will not dissolve, it will break or crack rather than crumble. If a modern hard cement is used when renovating old, soft brickwork, the tensions caused by thermal changes will often produce cracks — first in the mortar and eventually in the bricks themselves.

With an awareness of these properties, however, today's mason has a choice of those combinations that will most closely suit his needs. Once this decision has been made, he should also consider the still divergent opinions that surround the proper proportions for mixing a good mortar.

Mortar Mixtures

Much of the contention among masons today concerning the true proportions and working consistencies of mortar mixtures comes largely from personal habit and experience. For those who lack this experience, manufacturers print their recommendations on the back of each bag of cement. Published material is also available to the amateur with a technological bent who is interested in studying compressive strengths and stress load graphs before starting a job.

To mix mortar you will need three ingredients: cement, sand, and water. Some masons, as has been noted, add more lime. For masonry work you should use a fine grade sand (or one matched to an existing sample), free from impurities. Screening the sand before mixing it with the other ingredients will help separate out any foreign matter.

Many reputable masons recommend the following proportions:

For use with hard brick: mix ten (10) shovelsful of fine sand to one (1) bag of either light or dark masonry (mortar) cement. The color you choose will be determined by the desired appearance of the finished joints. This is about a 2:1 ratio of sand to cement. (To be more certain, use the same shovel to measure out your proportions of both sand and cement.)

Or, use one (1) bag of Portland cement, one (1) bag of hydrated (mason's) lime, and twenty (20) shovelsful of fine sand. This will also produce a 2:1 ratio of sand to cement/lime.

These proportions are frequently contested. Because of the ever-increasing strength of today's cement, most manufacturers recommend almost three (3) parts of sand to one (1) of mortar cement (or an equal amount of cement and lime). This would seem a more reasonable proportion to follow when using soft brick in the construction.

However, many leading architectural conservators throughout the country forcefully contend that most masons and manufacturers simply do not understand the problem. They stress that a lime-rich mortar is the only thing to use with soft bricks, i.e., one (1) part Portland cement; three (3) to six (6) parts hydrated lime; eight (8) to twelve (12) parts sand.

Finding a proper working consistency will only come from your experience or by looking over a mason's shoulder as he works. You should try for a mixture that is neither too wet (which will refuse to stay where you want it and slide down the face of the bricks) nor too dry (which will lump up and not allow you to bond the bricks tightly and evenly). The determinant is in the amount of water you add to the sand/cement mixture. It is always better to err on the side of too little water, then add more as you continue the mixing process. A too watery mixture can often be corrected by increasing the amount of sand and cement, but there will always be a question about proportions and, ultimately, its relative strength. One variable which often throws off the consistency however careful you have tried to be in your measurements may come from the amount of water already contained in the sand — especially if this has been stored outdoors and exposed to the weather.

Masonry Tools and Equipment

The most encouraging aspect of working with masonry is the small amount of equipment you will find necessary to do the job. Even if you wanted to update an ancient craft, there is very little leeway for making modern improvements. Laying brick can be a tedious and time-consuming business that demands patience on the part of both mason and homeowner to wait and give the mortar time to set before proceding with subsequent steps.

From the beginning you will need some means of mixing your mortar. This can be done by hand with a trowel in a metal bucket, in a mason's trough with a garden hoe or shovel, or in a gasoline- or electrically-powered cement mixer. If you do not already have one, mixers can be rented by the day from many local hardware stores or building supply companies. But unless you are already adept at laying bricks and know exactly what you are doing before you start the next step, the amount of mortar you will be able to use in one batch before it begins to set up will be relatively small. Therefore, for this type of project which will demand meticulous, slow work, the use of a mechanical mixer can reasonably be ruled out. It would be more practical — if you have a potential labor force at hand — and more educational as well to organize your helpers so that one mixes mortar (which will give a more consistent result) and another carries it to the site.

First, you should screen the sand. This will eliminate impurities and any oversized particles that both weaken the mortar and make laying bricks evenly more difficult.

You can buy a round, flat-bottomed strainer or sieve for this or make one yourself. The bottom is covered with a standard-sized wire mesh (usually forming a gridwork of either ¼" or ½" squares). Load the sieve with sand and jiggle it from side to side. Or, to process larger amounts at a time, buy a length of hardware cloth (despite the name, this is also a wire mesh of regular-sized squares) and staple it to a simple wooden frame. This larger strainer, usually rectangular in shape, can be elevated and propped up at one end. As shovelsful of sand are thrown against it at the top, the finer particles fall through while larger ones and debris bounce down the grid and accumulate at the bottom.

The actual mixing process will depend on the kind of equipment you have chosen to work with. It may require only such common tools as shovels, hoes, trowels, and sieves. In addition, you will need some containers in which to do the mixing and perhaps another to transport the mortar to the site. (For outdoor masonry work, a metal wheelbarrow is often the means of transportation; buckets will do as well for work indoors).

Mortar must be mixed thoroughly to attain its greatest strength. Combine the dry ingredients (sand, cement, and lime) first. Make sure the result is uniform without streaks. If using a bucket or trough, pile this dry mixture into a mound and make a depression in the top. Pour water into this. Use a trowel, hoe, or flat-ended shovel to draw the dry ingredients into the depression and mix them with the water. Repeat until all the water has been absorbed. Then add enough more to assure a mortar consistency that can be easily worked.

Mason's Tools

Before you can start to build your oven you should collect the following hand tools:

Brick Trowel or **Pointing Trowel** — These are flat, triangularly-shaped, stiff metal trowels with wooden handles. The brick trowel has a blade 10" long. It is used for scooping larger amounts of mortar from the batch to the bricks. The pointing trowel — with a blade 5½" long — is merely a smaller version. This is principally used for working the mortar into the joints after the bricks have been laid and for pointing in smaller areas. The butt end of the trowel handles are also used for tapping the bricks as they are set in mortar for accurate alignment.

Brick Jointers — These hand tools come in a variety of sizes and different widths. They are used to force mortar into the joints and smooth it out. There are several kinds of joints used in brickwork (concave, weathered, flush or rough-cut, V-shaped, and

40

Fig. 9. Fine old joints and recessed mortar are displayed by the closely set brick-work on the front wall of this brick oven. The rather sharply angled fireplace covings provide increased utilization of reflected heat.   Herbert L. Whitney photo

raked) but because a smooth surface is one of the major require-ments for the interior of the brick bake oven, the simple flush joint is the one most commonly used. This can be accomplished by using the trowel alone; however, a flat jointer will do a better job of forcing the mortar into the linear spaces and thus com-pressing it to form a tighter bond. For the front of the bake oven you may want to select one of the other jointers which will recess or angle the mortar and give more prominence to the brickwork.

Brick Set — This tool is a broad, flat metal chisel used for cut-ting bricks lengthwise when smaller pieces are needed to fit a par-

41

ticular space. The blade end is laid flat on the brick and the upper end tapped with a hammer. Because of the irregular composition of the bricks, practice is needed to perfect the ability to cut clean lines.

Brick Mason's Hammer — This wooden handled hammer is essential for any brickwork. The metal striking end is flat but its opposite end curved slightly towards the butt of the handle and is solid — unlike the clawed end of a carpenter's hammer. This end is also beveled and can be sharpened. As with the brick set, consistent accuracy in shaping bricks (usually cutting angles and lobbing off protrusions rather than making long cuts) can be obtained with this tool only after repeated practice. The mason holds his brick in one hand and strikes at it with the hammer held in the other. Short, hard confident raps will be more effective than a series of hesitant tappings.

Two Additional Pointers for Amateur Bricklayers

For those completely without experience in masonry work, here are two bits of information that, if observed, may save later frustration. For those with experience, these practices have become habitual. Both involve using water.

Bricks are porous, no matter at what temperature they have been fired. To prevent them from drawing up too much of the moisture in the mortar mixture as it is setting, soak your bricks before using them. This will allow the mortar a longer time to firm up and result in tighter, stronger bonds. One way of doing this is to have a large tub of water nearby in which to stack your bricks. As you deplete the supply, keep adding more to give you a continuous stock of pre-soaked bricks with which to work.

Water is also necessary for cleaning your tools. Although it will not harden immediately, mortar has a way of accumulating on tools if the mason is not alert. This adds to the weight and detracts from the accuracy of hand tools. After a batch of mortar has been mixed, hose off all equipment. Shovels and hoes should be scoured with sand and the mixing container turned over to drain. Trowels and jointers should also be cleaned thoroughly after each day's work and set up to dry, so that when the next session begins both the tools and the mason will be ready.

Constructing a Brick Bake Oven for the Home

By now you should be more than ready to begin construction. Since all brick bake ovens have some characteristics in common despite their style and location and age, here are some basic points to consider (see also Fig. 10):

1. The home-use oven has an approximate width of from 26" to 30" and a depth of from 26" to 40" depending on whether the hearth is essentially round or oblong. It is usually about 30" above the floor level.

2. The opening to the oven proper (whether it is to be covered with a wooden plank, a portable metal door, or a hinged, cast iron fitted door) is as small as possible while still allowing for the easy passage of food and fuel. This is from 14" to 18" wide and from 10" to 16" tall. The height is generally determined by the choice of a lintel or an arch. Arches are constructed of brick; lintels of dressed stone or an iron bar above which the brick courses rest. The opening of the lintel oven is always wider than it is tall to help prevent excessive heat loss when the oven is uncovered. Sometimes the dimensions of the opening will be determined by the type of covering that is planned, especially if this is to be a cast iron frame and door with a sliding damper arrangement. For the latter it is always easier to plan around standard sizes than to have something made to order later.

3. The oven hearth or floor is flat and paved with brick (usually set from front to rear in parallel rows) so hot coals can be raked out and containers of food inserted without the danger of their catching on protrusions and overturning. The hearth itself is supported by one or more large, flat stones or by stout hardwood planks whose ends have previously been embedded in the foundation walls beneath the oven proper. Such support for the floor is necessary because a floor of brick cannot be self-supporting. A more modern method of support is to construct a reinforced concrete pad on which to overlay your brick floor. This will involve building wooden forms, laying out a gridwork of corrugated steel reinforcing rods on top of the foundation walls, and filling in the forms with a rich Portland cement mixture.

4. The oven walls and dome are of double thickness with alternating joints. This not only helps retain heat but strengthens

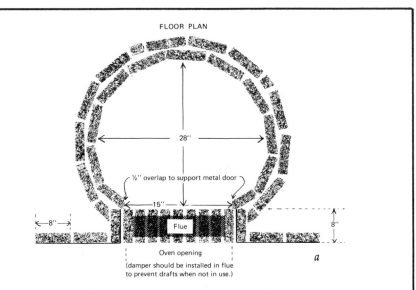

FLOOR PLAN

28"

½" overlap to support metal door

15"

8"

Flue

8"

Oven opening

(damper should be installed in flue
to prevent drafts when not in use.)

a

Fig. 10. Typical proportions for construction of a brick bake oven. *a* — Floor plan (above); *b* — front elevation (below); *c* — side cross-section (opposite page) of a corbelled dome. Though corbelling is the easier process, rolling is recommended for a smoother dome (see Figs. 11 and 15, *b*).

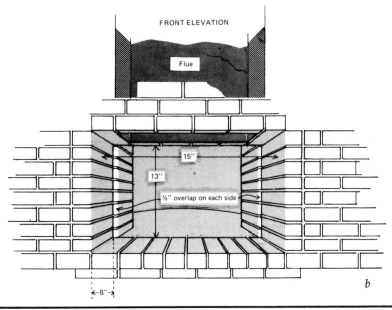

FRONT ELEVATION

Flue

15"

13"

½" overlap on each side

8"

b

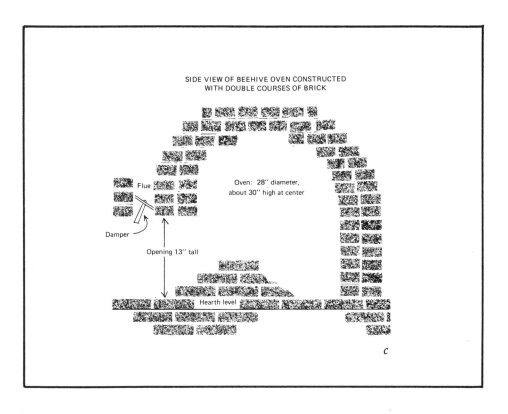

SIDE VIEW OF BEEHIVE OVEN CONSTRUCTED
WITH DOUBLE COURSES OF BRICK

Flue

Oven: 28″ diameter,
about 30″ high at center

Damper

Opening 13″ tall

Hearth level

c

the structure. It also will provide some protection against fire eating out the mortared joints and possibly reaching wooden partitions.

5. All interior surfaces of the oven must be laid as smoothly as possible to allow the heat to radiate effectively and to guard against soot accumulation. As little mortar as possible should be used between the inner joints; mortar is less resistant than brick to thermal change and may crack or crumble if large areas are left exposed. In forming the dome of the oven, bricks should be rolled rather than corbelled. This is a bit more difficult to do but the result will be smooth rather than a jagged series of courses. To roll a brick, tip it inwards longitudinally as it is laid. Apply a thicker bed of mortar to the outside edge of the previous course and just enough to the inner edge to assure a tight bond. The degree of roll becomes more pronounced with each subsequent course. The curve of the dome can be regulated if each course is completed entirely before another is started. (Corbelling, a method often used on the back wall of a fireplace where it is brought in to form the smoke shelf, is the technique of laying each course of brick with a slight longitudinal overlap rather than a roll. This reduces the size of the chimney area but retains the strength of the structure. It produces a jagged series of bricked courses rather than an evenly smooth wall.)

There are many local variations that can be studied for the initial stages of construction of the inner walls of the oven. Here are three:

a. For the first course, the bricks are laid up-ended around the perimeter rather than on their flat sides. When this has been completed, all later courses are set horizontally and eventually rolled as soon as the dome begins to take shape (Fig. 6, b).

b. Two courses of brick are first laid horizontally with alternating joints in a horseshoe pattern around the perimeter of the oven floor. Beginning with the third course, the bricks are rolled slightly to start forming the dome.

c. The first six courses are laid horizontally and vertically plumb. Beginning with the seventh, an accentuated roll is started (Fig. 11).

These three variations — and many more can be studied in different areas of New England — mainly cause a difference in the appearance of the inner walls of the oven and determine at what height to begin to form the dome. Each can result in ovens of the same height from hearth to capping. This dimension is controlled by the degree of roll incorporated in each course as it is laid. In example "c" — with higher vertical walls — the degree of roll is greater than for either "a" or "b" if the resulting oven is to occupy the same vertical space. Ovens with lower vertical walls and less pronounced roll as the dome begins to form will appear more squat perhaps but easier for the novice to build and even more structurally sound.

6. Some historians have suggested that wooden forms were used to create the uniform beehive shape of the brick bake oven. Presumably, these were made as a series of ribs — like those in a round-bottomed boat — reversed, assembled on the oven hearth, and tacked together. The brick courses were laid around the outside of this form. The result — when the form was either taken apart and removed through the oven opening or burned out after the oven had been completed — would be a uniform shape. If this method were used in earlier times, as far as is known none of the forms have been discovered. Perhaps in removing them they were so splintered they automatically served as kindling to test the draft of the new oven in a trial run.

Another kind of form is wet, packed sand. This was the method used by masons to construct the large, communal bake ovens in the Moravian settlement at Winston-Salem, North Carolina. A large pile of wet sand was dumped in the center of the brick oven hearth. As each course was mortared around the perimeter of the oven floor, sand was drawn in from the pile and packed tightly along the inner wall. The oven opening was boarded up to prevent the sand from leaking out. As the dome

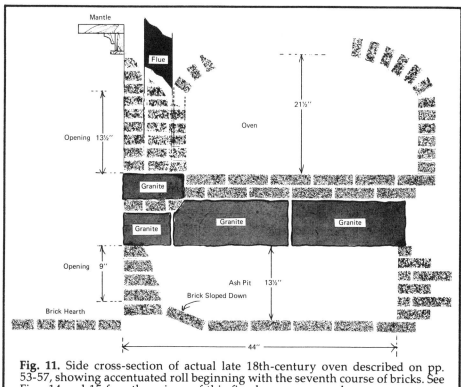

Fig. 11. Side cross-section of actual late 18th-century oven described on pp. 53-57, showing accentuated roll beginning with the seventh course of bricks. See Figs. 14 and 15 for other views of this fireplace-oven complex.

rose, more sand was added, kept wet, and forced in against the bricks to keep the rolled courses from collapsing. Once the cap had been mortared in place, the structure was left long enough for the bonding to set. Then the oven opening was unboarded and the sand — now dry — was scooped out and carted away. This left a structurally sound, dry brick dome.

According to masons who have had experience constructing many brick bake ovens in this century, a reliance on forms should not be necessary when building an oven on a home-use scale. Both wooden forms and sand will get in the way of smoothing the inner joints between the bricks before the mortar has set. Should the dome of a small oven threaten to collapse as it is being laid — which would be the principal reason for having to rely on support — scrap boards can be used to prop it up until the mortar has had a chance to harden, and then withdrawn through the oven opening. A threatened collapse may be caused by an improper mortar consistency (one that is either too wet or too dry), by too rich or too lean a mixture, or by the impatience of the mason who does not allow enough time for the mortar to begin to set up before he starts laying additional courses.

7. The facing of the brick bake oven can be constructed either concurrently with the sides and dome or after they have been completed. In either case, plans should be made from the beginning to leave enough room for the inclusion of a flue in front of the oven and above the opening (for an oven located in either of the fireplace jambs) and for the type of oven covering that is to be used.

In many old brick bake ovens the horseshoe pattern was used as a floor plan. The open end of the pattern was butted against and recessed 4" or more from each side of the oven opening. This often resulted in two areas on each side of the oven that were difficult to reach and therefore hard to clean out. The problem becomes greater the more the walls are recessed. Individual shaping of bricks, however, could be avoided with this method because the square ends of the courses which formed the walls were mortared against the flat inner sides of the facing bricks.

One way to overcome corners in the oven is to use a brick set and mason's hammer. (Beginners as well as experienced masons should remember that "mistakes" of judgment and execution in reshaping bricks can always be incorporated in the hidden outer

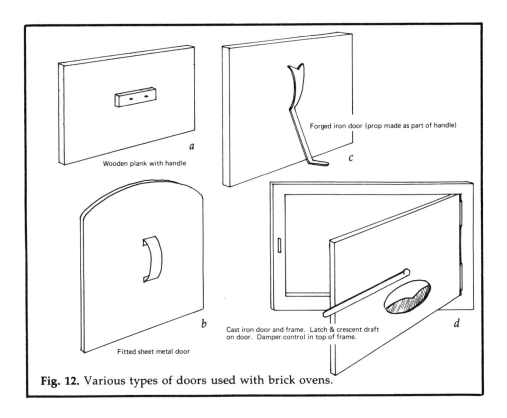

Fig. 12. Various types of doors used with brick ovens.

lining of the oven in case the pile of discards becomes so great as to be discouraging.) For this method the floor plan of the oven is more circular in shape. Angle off the corners of bricks that will abut the inner sides of the oven opening. Mortar the initial bricks in each course so that the acute angle of the wall brick is laid even with the squared end of the brick that forms the inner surface of the oven opening.

8. There are two ways to plan for the use of a portable oven door. The older method is to leave a vertical slot approximately 1" deep and taller than the oven opening between the oven-facing bricks and those set at right angles to form the front of the jamb itself (Fig. 3, c). One end of a door can slide into this groove to assure a close fit against the oven opening, the other can be propped in place. Another method is to construct a ½" brick lip on each side of the oven opening behind the facing bricks. A portable door can rest against these and can be reinforced with a diagonal prop leading to the oven hearth that is often part of the door handle itself (Fig. 12, c).

49

Cast iron doors and frames in standard sizes can still be bought in some hardware stores if you cannot find an appropriate old one. Temporarily prop the frame in place, and mortar coursed brick around it. To make sure the frame will be permanent, force additional mortar between the frame and the bricks on the inside surface and smooth the joints while the mortar is still workable.

9. One of the final steps in the construction of the brick bake oven will be the construction of a flue and damper by which to control heat and regulate combustion. If the oven is built into the back wall of the fireplace or into either of the covings, such a flue may not be necessary (although some do occur) because the oven can share the central chimney. However, when an oven is constructed in either of the fireplace jambs some accommodation must be provided to vent the smoke to the outdoors. The oven flue starts in front of and above the oven opening and connects with the fireplace flue unseen behind the chimney breast at about ceiling height. Today, in new construction you should use chimney flue tiles (a glazed ceramic product of various standard dimensions and usually tan to orange in color) — cut at angles where necessary — and mortared at the joints to assure tight bonds. For the oven flue these can be the 12" x 12" size. The first one is set in place after the lower end of the vent has been reduced with brick to a depth of 4" - 6" (front to rear) leaving the 12" width from side to side. Allow room to insert a standard-size damper; otherwise, you will have to have one custom-made and install it later. The damper can either be the swing type that pivots on a pin mortared at each end into the brickwork and operated by a handle which hangs down above the oven opening, or a sliding damper, the handle of which is inserted through a gap left in the facing bricks or a hole in the top of the cast iron door frame. The latter type operates horizontally from front to rear and rests on brick lips that have been left on both sides of the bottom of the vent before the first flue liner is installed.

10. After the walls and dome of the oven have been constructed with double layers of brick, you may want to add additional insulation. This will increase heat retention and provide a further buffer against the possibility of heat reaching the wooden partitions that surround the oven. Some early masons packed sand around the outer walls and dome, then plastered this over

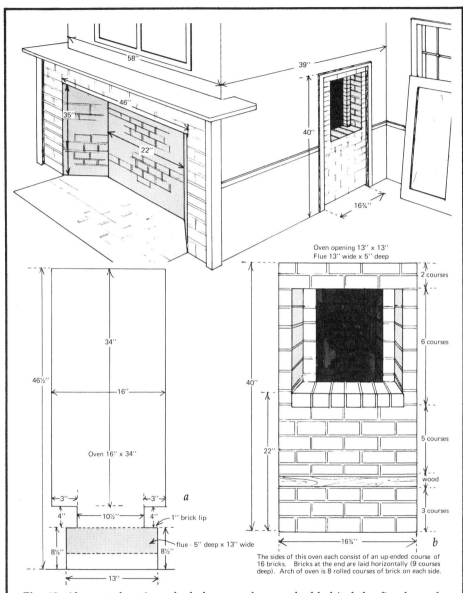

Oven opening 13" x 13"
Flue 13" wide x 5" deep

2 courses

6 courses

5 courses

wood

3 courses

Oven 16" x 34"

1" brick lip

flue - 5" deep x 13" wide

a

b

The sides of this oven each consist of an up-ended course of
16 bricks.   Bricks at the end are laid horizontally (9 courses
deep).   Arch of oven is 8 rolled courses of brick on each side.

Fig. 13. Alternate location of a bake oven, here tucked behind the fireplace of a
house built *c.* 1770-1780. The oven is covered when not in use by the wooden
panel leaning up against the window. *a* — Floor plan and *b* — front elevation of
oven.

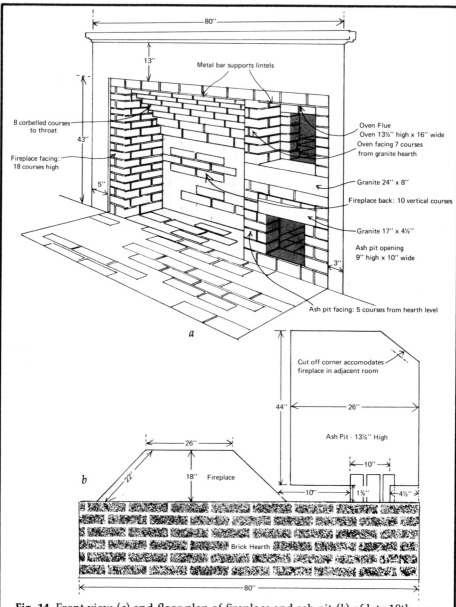

Fig. 14. Front view (*a*) and floor plan of fireplace and ash pit (*b*) of late 18th-century oven complex described on pp. 53-57. (See also Figs. 11 and 15.)

with another coating of clay or cement. Today, some pack cut stone over the dome to act as insulation.

Miss Beecher's *Domestic Receipt-Book,* designed as a supplement to her *Treatise on Domestic Economy* of 1846, published by Harper & Brothers, New York, suggests a third method of providing this insulation:

"The best ovens are usually made thus. After the arch is formed, four or five bushels of ashes are spread over it, and then a covering of charcoal over that, then another layer of bricks overall. The use of this is, that the ashes become heated, and the charcoal being a non-conductor, the heat is retained much longer."

11. As a final observation about the general characteristics of typical bake ovens, it should be noted that there is no reason why an oven must be built adjacent to — or even in conjunction with — a fireplace today. In the pre-stove era the two went side-by-side as a matter of convenience. This was also a way of consolidating building material and saving labor. However, as long as an oven flue can be accomodated, this simple structure could conceivably be built anywhere in today's kitchen or in an ell or outbuilding as an independent unit. Custom dictated the location of the bake oven; today's needs may be enough to spark the individual homeowner to relocate the brick bake oven to suit his own convenience. This, then, could be interpreted as just another step in the normal evolution of the oven.

Recreating a Late-18th Century Home Brick Bake Oven Today

We hope you have already gleaned from your reading that there are probably as many variations in home brick bake ovens in old houses today as there were masons who built them and housewives who dictated their design and placement. Given the tools, a few pointers, and some natural dexterity, anyone who is willing to take the time can either copy an extant oven or build a functional one that is even more individualistic.

Here follow detailed plans of an oven that was built in the late 1700s (Figs. 11, 14, and 15). Dimensions are provided but if these are taken literally and modern brick used instead of old, the measurements will vary slightly. Other changes may also occur. If dressed granite is not available for your oven, authenticity may have to be sacrificed and substitutions made. An iron bar support for a bricked lintel will be less expensive. So will hardwood planks in place of the granite slabs that form the roof of the ash pit.

This brick bake oven has a separate flue but no damper. To update this arrangement see Paragraph 9 (p. 50). This example was chosen as an illustration because it is adjacent to a typical kitchen fireplace; it is as safe to use as any wood-fired bake oven, and it contains a cavity for the storage of harmless ashes which also minimizes the amount of masonry needed to bring the oven hearth up to working height. All of these are characteristic of the cooking arrangements after the American Revolution and before the 19th century got into full swing.

(Incidentally, in the house from which this example was taken, there is an identical brick-oven/fireplace complex in the cellar directly below this one. It is interesting to speculate whether cooking in that household was at one time socially elevated to its present first floor accommodation or whether the growing needs of the family of the time demanded that a second facility be built in the cellar at a later date. So far as is known, there is no documentation to support one theory or the other.)

If such an oven were to be copied today, here are the steps that must be taken:

A. The Foundation and Footing — To give solid support for the sheer mass and weight of the masonry above it, an ample foundation and footing must be provided. In many early American houses which boast a central chimney through which from three to five fireplaces were vented (Fig. 8), the chimney foundation was laid up in the cellar with fieldstone and boulders but without mortar. This formed a massive cube of rubble stretching from the cellar floor to the ceiling. Sometimes this core was made of dressed stone and filled with dry rubble. In other houses — to lessen the amount of fill needed and to provide a useful additional storage space for food and utensils — a bricked arch was constructed within the chimney core. This was either an open-ended tunnel or enclosed at one end to form a cul-de-sac.

Whatever method is used in today's house — and most likely it will involve poured concrete or a cement block construction — the important point to remember is that the foundation and footing be sturdy enough to support the weight above it and have a relatively flat surface by the time it pokes through the first floor. Local building codes can be consulted to establish required dimensions. Once the footing and foundation have been built, you will be ready to plan first for the ash pit and later for the oven itself.

(In the case of renovation work, if a rubble core foundation already exists in your house and you intend to build a bake oven, you should first pour a reinforced 4" concrete pad on top of it to make a strong, level area to start with. First, pack gravel on the rubble. Then build forms around the area of slightly larger dimensions than your ash pit floor. Set the reinforcing rods and pour a pad using a mixture of Portland cement. Float the top of the pad while the mixture can still be worked until it is level with the tops of the forms.)

B. The Ash Pit Floor — Because live coals will not be stored in this cavity (and if it is built on a level cement pad), there is no need for more than one course of bricks to form the floor of the ash pit. Even this will be largely for the sake of appearance. The brick should be laid in parallel courses from front to rear with mortar cement and the joints well pointed. This arrangement will leave fewer ridges on the floor and make it easier to remove the ashes with a shovel. In this example, the second row of bricks was sloped down towards the back when the floor was built so that most of the area is one course of brick lower than the level of the hearth. Presumably, this was an accommodation made by the mason on the spot either to increase the capacity of the ash pit or to correct a misjudgment in the level of the foundation and prevent a brick-deep lip being left across the width of the floor. This variation does not occur in the similar ash pit in the cellar.

C. The Walls of the Ash Pit — The ash pit opening is 10" wide and 9" high. The piers consist of five (5) courses of brick from the level of the fireplace hearth. The lowest course doubles as the ash pit floor and front of the hearth. Because of the row of sloping bricks, the side walls and back include an extra course to make it a cavity 13½" high, 26" wide, and 44" deep. The back right-hand corner has been angled to conform to the fireplace coving in an adjoining room.

D. The Ash Pit Roof — Dressed granite was used to form the roof and support the floor of the bake oven. Two slabs — approx-

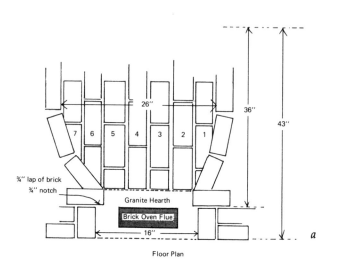

Floor Plan

Brick floor of oven - numbered right to left shows oven is offset to left. Numbers 2,3,4 and 5 line up directly with oven opening. Numbers 1,6 and 7 are behind facing bricks.

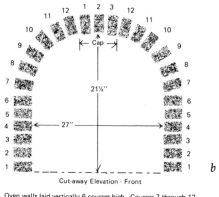

Cut-away Elevation · Front

Oven walls laid vertically 6 courses high. Courses 7 through 12 "rolled" to make dome. Final 3 rolled courses cap dome.

Fig. 15. Two more views of oven described on pp. 53-57. *a* — Oven floor plan, showing how the oven was slightly offset to the left to use all available space; *b* — frontal cross-section, cut away to show oven dome and rolled courses. (See also Figs. 11 and 14.)

imately 30" long and 18" wide — span the vertically plumb ash pit walls. A third, lesser piece — 17" x 8" x 4½" — forms the lintel. Apparently because this was thinner than the other slabs, some adjustments were made to bring them all up to the same level. A single course of brick was laid on the lintel stone. This may have been done for other reasons as well: the brick course makes a visual break between granite slabs and acts as a cushion; stone displaced the use of a large number of bricks.

E. The Oven Hearth — The hearth is constructed of two courses of brick set in mortar on top of the ash pit roof. With alternating, well-pointed joints, this minimizes the danger of escaping fire. It also provides for better heat retention. This oven is slightly offset to the left to make use of all available space (Fig. 15, *a*). The oven floor consists of seven (7) parallel rows of brick laid flat from front to rear. Courses 2, 3, 4, & 5 line up with the 14½" wide opening. The distance between the brick piers under the flue has been increased to 16". The difference is accounted for by the two ¾" vertical brick lips and grooves left to accommodate a portable oven door. Rows 1, 6, & 7 are behind the facing bricks and partly covered at each end by the positioning of the oven walls.

F. Walls and Dome — The walls consist of six (6) courses of brick laid horizontally so that the inner vertical surface is smooth and plumb. The floor area (26" across at its broadest, 36" deep from where the door is positioned) is an offset oval, the front end of which has been sliced off to allow for the oven opening. Instead of using the horseshoe pattern, here the mason angled off the ends of the near bricks in each course so they would fit flush against the inner surface of the facing bricks, leaving areas that are accessible to peel and broom. The seventh course is rolled with the degree of roll increasing through the twelfth. The oven cap — relatively flat and extending from front to rear — consists of three final courses bringing the height of the beehive dome to 21½" from the hearth (Fig. 15, *b*).

Fig. 16. Cooking in a brick bake oven is a real challenge today, but it certainly can be done, as this pie, freshly baked in January, 1977 in the Pliny Freeman farmhouse of Old Sturbridge Village bake oven testifies.

Stephen T. Whitney photo (Courtesy Old Sturbridge Village, Sturbridge, Massachusetts)

Using the Brick Bake Oven 3

The most common questions asked by visitors to restored villages in New England where demonstrations of home baking are part of on-going educational programs involve the use rather than the construction of the brick bake oven.

Ultimately, whether one is thinking of restoring an old oven or building a new one — or is just idly curious — the object in having one is to know how to operate it. A little information can be gleaned from out-of-date publications in the library, and some from the memories of older people who remember seeing ovens used when they were children, but more helpful is to see baking actually in process and to question first hand those carrying it out.

Two questions frequently recur: Where is the fire made? How much wood does it take?

By the kinds of construction discussed in this book for early American brick bake ovens, it is obvious that the fire is built on the bricked hearth of the oven itself. (Some evidence indicates that owners of old ovens may have experimented by starting a fire in the lower opening — the ash pit — without having first thought to check the construction of the roof or to wonder how the smoke and flames are to be vented to the outdoors. Such experiments undoubtedly account for the charring of the planked ash pit roof and may even have led to destruction of the house itself.) When sufficient heat has been generated in the oven, the remaining coals and ashes are removed, the oven is cleaned, food inserted, and a door propped against the oven opening to retain the heat during baking. If properly done, baking of assorted foods can continue for hours without need for additional heat.

Estimates of the wood consumed in this operation have ranged from ¼ to a full cord — 128 cubic feet — enough to discourage anyone seriously interested in restoring the home baking process in a wood-fired oven.

It must be granted that every cook and oven may have different requirements, that the amount of heat needed will depend on the volume of the particular oven and the amount of heat generated will depend on the kinds of wood used and their stage of seasoning. Nevertheless, some shortcuts and innovations have always been found by ingenious cooks with experience. While a brick bake oven is certainly more complicated to operate than a modern range oven — and more time-consuming — it is not as difficult or as hungry for wood as the most dire warnings suggest.

Miss Beecher — referred to on p. 53 — had this to say in her advice of a century and a quarter ago:

"The first time an oven is used, it should be heated the day previous for half a day, and the oven lid kept up after the fire is out, till heated for baking.

"As there is so little discretion to be found in those who heat ovens, the housekeeper will save much trouble and mortification by this arrangement. Have oven wood prepared of sticks of equal size and length. Find, by trial, just how many are required to heat the oven, and then require just that number be used and no more."

(The author's frugality is apparent. So, too, is a then prevalent attitude concerning domestic help. Miss Beecher was not unique in feeling that hired girls were naturally wasteful of their employer's resources as well as lacking in enough native intelligence to be left to their own devices.)

There are some today who say that only live coals — not kindling and oven wood — were used to heat the dome-shaped oven. This may have been possible when the kitchen fireplace was continuously burning and coals readily available. It is more likely that coals alone were used only as an expedient to prepare a single item of food or warm left-overs. This would save time and fuel firing up the oven to the necessary temperatures for day-long or overnight baking of many different dishes.

Those who use brick ovens now follow part of Miss Beecher's advice whether or not they are aware of it: through experience they have found the amount of wood necessary to heat their oven ("about an armload of split, dry hardwood for all-day baking," one modern practitioner with seventeen years experience suggests) and, therefore, have a personal guideline by which to judge the fuel to help achieve consistent temperatures day in and day out. They also have their woodshed arranged so one section is reserved for oven wood (maple, oak, beech, birch, etc.), cut to the proper length and well-seasoned. This practice saves time and increases efficiency.

To heat the oven, place several handsful of kindling (pine shavings, twigs, slivered boards, etc.) on the oven floor. Miss Beecher says the fire must be made at the back of the oven; however, combustion and heat radiation will be just as effective if it is laid in the center of the oven and it will be more convenient to reach. Next, stack your armload of oven wood cob-wise on top of it and light the fire. Once you are sure it has caught properly, prop the cover lightly against the opening to allow a supply of fresh air to be drawn into the oven and the smoke to escape up the flue. After the fire has burned down some, close the oven door to help retain the heat in the bricks and reduce the wood to live coals.

To heat a home bake oven will take from 1½ to 2 hours. This will give the cook time to prepare the food. It is better to feed your whole quota of wood into the oven at the beginning although more can be added if it has taken longer to get the food ready than anticipated and the oven is cooling. Remember, however, the more the oven door is opened, the less heat will be retained.

Food is baked on retained heat. It is always better to overheat the brick oven and allow it to cool down to the desired cooking temperature. Otherwise, you will have to rekindle a fire and begin the whole process again. Before inserting food, coals and ashes must be removed and the oven floor cleaned.

Miss Beecher says, ". . . the oven must be heated so hot as to allow it to be closed fifteen minutes after clearing, before heat is reduced enough to use it. This is called *soaking*. If it is burnt down entirely to ashes, the oven may be used as soon as cleared."

To remove the coals use a metal peel or oven rake. A long-handled hoe is sometimes used to draw the coals forward and a small ash shovel to extract them. *Do not throw live coals in the ash pit.* Pile them in one corner of the fireplace until they become harmless. To clean the oven hearth of ash residue, use a water-soaked broom. Early cooks often kept a dried turkey wing on the mantle shelf to accomplish this.

Work to ready the oven as quickly as possible in order to conserve the heat. Today an oven thermometer can be used to tell you how hot the oven is. Otherwise, you will have to depend on your own experience. There are some traditional methods to tell when the oven is ready:

1. The bricks must all look red. If black spots are not all burnt off, it is not hot enough.

2. Sprinkle flour on the oven hearth. If it burns black right away, the oven is too hot.

3. Insert the tender part of your wrist towards the inner corners of the oven behind the front walls and count. If you cannot hold your hand in longer than to count to twenty moderately, it is hot enough. If you can count to thirty moderately, it is not hot enough for bread.

The counting suggestions will not work the same for all cooks, some being more sensitive to heat than others. Among those who operate brick ovens today, the consensus is that each cook must know her own oven, her fuel, and be able to adjust its performance according to the results of her baking.

The advantage the brick oven has over one of its predecessors, the Dutch oven, is that its use will result in increased quantity baked at one time, and considerably more variety. Some foods must be prepared the night before; bread must have time to rise; beans for baking must be pre-soaked, etc. Those foods which take the longest to bake are inserted on a metal peel at the back of the oven. Those that take the least time are placed near the front. All food need not be put into the oven at the same time, of course. Here, again, experience will determine the timing. Properly heated, the oven will continue to radiate heat for most of the day — from early morning until late in the afternoon — on one firing. If too much heat loss has occurred in the final hour of baking a pot of beans, for example, supplemental heat can be provided by banking the pot with live coals, much as one does with a Dutch oven.

Once you have constructed a beehive bake oven — or reconditioned an old one — the real challenge will come in learning how to cook in it. Although tips can be gotten from people who use them today, the cook and her oven will have to learn each other's idiosyncracies until they each are functioning properly. It may well be the beginning of a permanent relationship.

THE END

Fig. 17. This late 18th-century brick oven-kitchen fireplace complex has been carefully restored and furnished with kitchen utensils of the period. (See Fig. 8 for detailed diagrams of the structure.)

Stephen T. Whitney photo